FEASTS OF EVASION

Larry D. Thacker

FUTURECYCLE PRESS
www.futurecycle.org

Cover artwork, a photocomposition by Diane Kistner from the photo "Dream: Orb and Canary" by Larry D. Thacker; author photo by the author; cover and interior book design by Diane Kistner; Georgia text and Philospher titling

Library of Congress Control Number: 2019939041

Published by FutureCycle Press
Athens, GA, USA

ISBN 978-1-942371-92-2

"Such minor Armageddons.
Beside the waters of disremembering,
I lay me down."

—Charles Wright
"Basic Dialogue," *Appalachia*

For those who run off,
yet hear a thing remaining.

Contents

First, Let's Admit We Don't Know Everything

That two eyes and ears and two hemispheres
of a brain aren't enough. That to see
the world behind us is to abandon the one
we've turned from, and if repeated,
is the discovery of a spinning blur of reason
we mistake as perception.
                              We have a chime
hanging past the glass doors. Light enough
for any breeze to sway, but not set to music,
heavy enough for finches to hold upon.
By the time I see one, it's only a streak
of tail feathers, the bird rested, taking flight.
But the chimes are now swinging and jingled,
and this is what has turned my attention.

Not a bird, but movement outside myself,
an instinctive shift of attention we might
call curiosity within the trick of civilization.

Second, let's admit we don't
                              want to know
everything. That the intoxication of spinning
keeps us returning to the well of curiosity.

That it's better for a third eye to be invisible
and for no one to have an answer
for where a third ear prefers hearing the world,
for sixth senses to remain argued theories.
That while we have seen birds in our lifetime,
the one we didn't see fully
may not have been a bird at all.

The Way In

to the dead

A shared cup of coffee, a plain brand,
quietly percolates on an early Saturday morning
when it seems nothing stirs but absolutes
at the table we share in the kitchen along
with the few evasive summer crickets.
A passing comment on how fast the grass
has grown since a last cutting, or
where the yard is dying in spots from drought.
A missed call from an unknown number, but
pondering a little too much on who it was
and what they wanted. Standing at the tea section
of the grocery store, knowing you'll very likely
get what you always do, but still bogging down
in the hundred choices, verging on tears, by a mystery
of something always creeping up on you
about now. Waking up at the keyboard, stunned,
to a string of forehead-typed letters, but feeling
there's a message in there somewhere if you'll only listen
for once. Heating up that untouched cup of coffee
on the other side of the kitchen table after watching
it cool, after placing it intentionally on those words
of the morning paper. Wondering what they have to say.

Enter the Feasts

Ocular: Gradually
I can't see the first half
of each new line I type.
A dark spot grows.
　　　　In the periphery.

What has died in the eye,
in and of the vision, collapsed,
allowing nothing to escape
the event horizon?

Then looking down at my fingers,
typing, most of my left hand
　　　　goes missing,

slowly, in an elongating

stringed mix of dull blankness

that eats light
　　　　next door
　　　　to strange
　　　　strobing stitches
　　　　of pulsated
　　　　lightning.

And the Lord went before them by day
in a pillar of a cloud, to lead them the way;
and by night in a pillar of fire, to give
them light; to go by day and night.

I thought I was having a stroke
the first time it happened.
I was in a music store talking guitars.

The salesman's face vanished,
starting with a pinhole blank grayness
following wherever I glanced.
It grew to cover half my sight field
before the streaks of light chimed in.

I kept talking through it, curious,
but paranoid I was about to experience
something terrible that never came.

A symptom of TIA
can include TMB,
not to be confused
with signs of TMJ,
nevertheless one
should call 911,
since a CT, MRI,
or EKG at the ER
may be in order.

It hit once while I was driving.
I was mostly blind. I merged
into the next town, waiting
it out in the first fast food
parking lot I could find.
I think it was a Wendy's.

"What are these peripheral hallucinations?"

Google whatever you imagine ails you
and someone out there suffers with you.
Take your pick from the forum:

A side-effect of some medicine, or
"floaters," or fringe hallucinations
shared by bipolar sufferers, or
little spirit animals in the shadow, or
demons in the periphery
                always there.

But then gone, like a good ghost.

Orb: A solid or semi-transparent sphere,
       usually manifesting in flash photography,
       caused when particles, such as dust,
       are caught up in light. Often claimed
       as indications of a spirit presence.

More like a lasting glow.
In the blinking, playing hide-and-seek
behind the lids, detached
from the day, never in direct view.

What needs be seen flees, clarity
consumed:
              A feast no one outlasts.

In Timing

I wedged my fingers into the slats
of the blinds and widened some light in

just as the first blasts of train horn
hit town, timing things as if the dying

wild grape vines in the tree line,
made just real in that sudden vision,

were singing a single preferred note
in the morning's rain storm. We live

just close enough to the train line
for them to haunt in on our routine,

just like this, paralleling our moves
by surprise, a spare voice at home,

even if we're not, watching over things,
probably singing along with the radio

or television, as attuned to the songs
as any twice-correct dead watch

might hope for in a good day's work.

Composition Goods

I'm walking the perimeter of a landfill
    in search of first lines of poems I've not started.
Television cabinet sans television, damaged: Abandoned
    on roadside with other furniture left behind
    by a paranoid, rent-evading couple, cabinet
    having once served as the base of a make-shift
    lemonade stand table along with a tossed door.
Dog carcass, mostly hide: Buried in the bottom
    of a kitchen trash can liner by a guilty feeling
    father after finding the family dog dead in its bed
    after the kids left for school. In his good suit
    and in too big a hurry to bury it in the back yard,
    he lied later. Told the kids that Okie ran away.
Plastic milk jug, crushed: Smashed by hand by a father
    who ran out of milk in the middle of a hurried
    breakfast worrying about getting the trash out
    and aligned perfectly with the curb on time.
A dented toaster, strung-out plug: Like a percentage
    of marriages, the arrangement was time-limited,
    manufactured with soon-to-be-faulty materials
    that can never last. One day it all just failed.
    That's what Janie told Andy when she came home:
    "It's just not working anymore, dear. It's time."
Dead seagull: Fresh, plump. Not even a hungry fly on it yet.
    Eye still glassy in the sun. Beak with a tear of plastic
    hanging out. Bellying up to the all-you-can-eat
    buffet catches up with you before long.
    A feather lifts in the wind's constant stink.
Erupted black bag of clothing, full of men's suit coats,
    slacks, a pair of mismatched dress shoes: Simply.
Two-by-four fragments: A tiny sample from a disaster
    area cleanup from a flood or hurricane or a tornado,
    shipped from another state's overwhelmed landfill.
School notebook, portion: Full of angsty poetry about
    a lost dog, a lost boyfriend, and lost virginity, all
    in the mood of the late Prince's album, *Purple Rain*.
Mannequin hand, left-handed: Missing middle finger.

Cicada, Thunder, & Train Spell

Treetops fan about like arguing hands,
an odd chosen few on one side of the house
in a twist with some portion of wind
yet reaching the next block,
treetops there remaining still,

not knowing they wait; it's all a constant
decision-making on something's part.
Thunder commences in the west

behind me, slow rolling, ambient flashes
rumored in. The east still dressed in evening blue,
dancing static brewing cicadas down
to a quietness with each growing crack
of thunder tumble in the valley,
all a sky soup sweeping a train through.

So it's another night
of thunder, train horn, and cicada song,
then a Harley stuttering along,
but with a firetruck siren this time,
and the wait for a run of first splats on car hoods
and the sidewalk warmth,
the press of wind finally
cooling through the porch eaves,

a glance of birds high,
caught in plummets,
fighting for perch.

There's the chime now and the fencerow shift
of thick vine, a leaf or two,

slightest yellowing in them, strobed
by another flash in the wheel of cloud.

Justness

We watch the grapevine in its wildness
spread all the heated season, a spindling
growth being large enough finally to birth

a mind, surely, by early August
as the evening winds are regular and move
the thing as one largeness, heaped over the fence-line

trees, swaying, frightening at a distance. What
has summer wrought, there across the field?
There, coming closer? Or do we only

fear what we deserve this time of year?

A Few More Questions

after W. S. Merwin

What is the head
> A box of black and white photos unnamed
> in an antique store a sad thing really
> and too expensive to take home whole

What are the fingertips
> Cold cold cold forgotten once

What of the arms
> They eventually dry and expand after
> the fresh body emerges from nymph form

What are the teeth
> Delicate tombstones alphabetical red bows

No what are the teeth I ask
> Sacrifices drawn down into anxious soil

What are the toes
> A way into dream structure one at a time
> feeling out out carefully onto the ice creek

What is the bone structure
> It is always laundry day when the sun's out
> and the wind blows lightly over your neck

What are the dreams
> The same box

What is in the mailbox
> Delivered after you filled out
> change of address forms twice

What was on the road back home
> A deer in headlights and a sickening thump
> you'd always imagined but you didn't stop no
> you went on home and went straight into
> the house and had breakfast the next morning
> without looking out into the driveway

An Enduring

The forest floor collapsed
under my step, emptied

of something vital, essential
like simple air, a breath,

or as if it was fashioned up
by some years of dried mothwing,

even the ground beneath
sighing as moss carpet

in wait for enough pressure
to bring it all lower, but softly,

quiet in a sweet disintegration,
imprinted there by my heavied boot,

the black and hollow of rotten log
abruptly wanting of a bridge

for two worlds, pressed, twinned,
a forest wholly changed.

Following, Downhill

First with sound.
Withholding breath, toes turned
down, digging in to hold
and freeze with moss.

Wave only like a branch, no more
noise than this so as to hear
where the stream hums its bending.

Turn the ear
where stones heat
in the sun, longing
for bare feet to pad over, but
only until the rains

from afar
melt them again down
into the all-waters.

Listen, and go.
Without hurry.
Without wanting.
There is sun still to use.

Second with touch.
A toe. Another. Then heel.
The crawlings. No twitch.

A rivering of itch-sweat down the spine.
Hold mist and fern in your
fingers, as best you can, up to the lips,
smacking the taste of want
from the air.

Without haste. Or need.
There is sun, still.
Off the hill of pine roots,
carpet of needle, soft. Forever there.

A thing better named than gravity
calling, voiced by the rock scatter.
Whitish water and bubble.

Green pull of water moss and thread,
inertial with globe-spin.

Follow on and lower. In trust.
Rock stumble and branch strip,
bark call, lichen glow in sun failing.

Something's lights flicker. Beyond
focus. A rumor of hope.
But a glow hovers like a near
aurora cloud, barely
calling. A hope, down
and hard on the legs.

Off the mountain. Animal
trail and moth flight, water sound.
Moon-sprinkle on ice glass.
The blue glow of lore. Story.

Third with spirit.
No sleep. Only trudge and memory.
Eyes probably open. Limbs
probably extended, into the grope.

Then, after a time, is that
laughter? A window of yellow light.
Flinch of warm movement.
Dog alarm.

Yes, always follow
            water downhill.
Even into a cold,
            unknown town of strangers.

Nightly

The nightly train horn cries
out under cooling clouds,
through newly naked trees, echoing
off building brick and hills
a novel dissonance.

We've turned our clocks back, confused
sound it would seem, as if two
trains warn one another
on the shared, trusted track.

A terribleness coming. Or
is this earth sounding, vibrating up
the hill, searching the few feet
of those who yet believe such things.

Whatever the animal, it feasts
on evasion from the senses,
on never giving up that curiosity,

of what such a wreckage of life
could be like.

But waits. For fear
of never having the crowd in the night
it was promised. Longs for.

For fear
of no one understanding
obscured language, echoed,

an hour delayed.

Of unexpected light.

A Change of Plans

I have lost my easy God—the one whose name
I knew since childhood.

                                        —James Kavanaugh

As I was taught at a young age, with pat little clichés
strong enough, I imagine, to still echo off the cement block
Sunday School walls of home, God has a plan
for everything: So I watch the shaky footage of a sniper
firing down into a crowd of 20,000 country music fans
and seek out the visage of God in the confusion and horror,
the scattering little children, men, women—some bleeding,
some very still, some running or limping cover-to-cover,
some soon to be still, some standing tall in the center
of danger, catching glimpses of something akin to another
sort of terror: a sudden sheer absence of youthful memory,
of early assurances, given all these panicked offspring
of the Almighty, though the Thousand Names of God
come naturally screaming—and not in worshipful prayer—
from the awful throats of the night's randomly chosen.

Vital Records

My birth certificate is missing. Gone. Vanished. I told the DMV I was obviously alive, having stood in line for over an hour, standing there speaking to them in need of another driver's license after moving from another state. I was sent away empty-handed. And now I've looked everywhere. Under things. Within things. On top of things. Around things. Beside things. Outside of things. At the end and at the beginning of things. In the middle. During pauses. I've searched for it, like hunting for my own voice, physically and philosophically. Emotionally. Existentially, though I probably should have begun there. I've asked family, friends. Acquaintances. Re-friended a few people on social media and mended feelings just in case. I've accosted strangers. I've accused the innocent. I've checked my person. My pockets, wallet. I've stared at all the mirrors I can find and mouthed the question over and over: Where am I?

An Incessancy of Morning

My writing room sits connected to the front porch,
my desk at a window. Along the middle of the dog days
of August, when I was up very early and writing, when
the day stayed quiet, I suffered recently from what I thought
was a ringing in my ears for a time, not too loudly,
but aggravating enough if I gave it much thought. But,

of course, that wasn't it at all. It was only outside calling in.
The sounding was that morning throng, crickets and frogs,
pitched high as to be a single note, much like a tinnitus
of nature searching the senses, vibrating through the windows
and walls. A mystery once solved I could ignore even less.

An Endurance II

For the sake of new trees, as if they crave a better view,
growing out of third-story abandoned buildings
along a dying Main Street, we endure.

For the sake of fog pooled in mud puddles and birdbaths
and sunken graves and dammed streams, we endure.

For the sake of scarlet hurricane sunrises
four-hundred miles from a coastline, we endure.

For the sake of cemetery shade from one surviving tree, we endure.

For the sake of Christmas trees left up
all year long, just because, we endure.

For the sake of random highway-shoulder yard sales
full of your history, we endure.

For the sake of spider webs glass-pearled with dew,
defying morning storm winds, we endure.

For the sake of random furniture on the side of the road
abandoned by families fleeing collection of back rent
from slumlord properties, we endure.

For the sake of a church on every fourth block, we endure.

For the sake of river pools deep enough to submerge a body,
    we endure.

For the sake of five-minute visits by a string of visitors
across the street at the obvious pill dealer's apartment
at the first of the month, we endure.

For the sake of dried mud on your dress shoes
from carrying your cousin's body up a hill to a fresh hole
in the ground, we endure.

For the sake of uninformed bees, we endure.

For the sake of slick scales tightening on scarred forearms and wrists,
    we endure.

For the sake of songs sung from mouths lost in the hilly woods,
    we endure.

The Invitation

I was at a 4th of July party at a faculty member's home recently.
We'd gotten there in the middle of a bad storm, sharing umbrellas,
dashing from tree to tree for relief when the hail came, but finally
settling in at the house, everyone drying off, suddenly with food
in hand, beers, the din of conversation filling to the high ceilings
and taking over the tap and whip of rain and wind outside.
So normal.

      Then I lose something. Find myself pacing between
cliques gathering up, their well-meaning noise too much, shutting
something off inside me. I'm off standing still, observing myself,
only a thin thought from believing I've ghosted myself accidentally
while staring down at the hummus and pita chips. I panic, but
I'm a little relieved. My appetite gone, I look around to consider
our hosts' old home, and whether I'd like it here, and I wander a bit
upstairs to see what's going on, make judgement on their choices
of furniture and color tones. I stroll the garden. Are those annuals
or perennials? Check for potential draftiness come winter. Try
the front porch swing. I love porches and swings. Check the mail.
See that it's stopped raining. The party's saved.

      Someone asks
what I've been writing lately. *Poems about the dead,* I respond.
Oh, they reply, and nothing follows as they drop a pita chip on
the nice oriental carpet. *Don't worry,* I'm tempted to assure them.
      I'll pick that up tonight long after everyone's gone.

To Watch the Poet Read

My game was jousting with the abstract expressionist poets,
    not with some imagined *them,* but with the difficulty:
    angrily interpreting their work, as if it was work,
    rather than someone's language of a lifetime.

I was angered, rather, with that hyper-self-awareness
    of likes and dislikes, self-made undercurrents of reasoned
    inner workings, holding off on what I might be able to do
    to make it all better for myself, easier, which I might
    or might not have wanted: why would one want to enjoy
    everything one reads?
                    No one's that reasonable.

It would be behind the eyes, I sensed. What isn't?

I searched out footage of their readings and interviews.
    Not for words, but for their souls: those things
    we're never supposed to speak of, you know, unless
    indirectly and metaphorically and quite brilliantly. Yet,
    there they were, behind the tick-tock glassy knowing,
    all-knowing. Waiting on my poor little epiphany.

Maybe it was all the old poets, for all I knew, not only
    the celebrated absurdists blazing through their abstractions.
    Is anything more heartbreaking than the eyes of the aging poet
    when speaking of their work of life, or when reading?
    Begging: *Time, more time.*
                    We've almost got it.

You and I. Nearly.
        If only we might puzzle up
these few more lines of the everyday and every night. Turn
the mundane to gold, even as fools.
        Together this time.

There's an endgame down in the difficulty,
        I swear it.

I Felt a Brush Across My Arm as I Stepped Onto the Porch

Nothing more than a hair's touch, but enough to sense
I'd disturbed the near invisibleness of a spider's web,

quickly brushing off my forearm and elbow. I shifted, stood
just right by the sun and found the web in its perfection,

now cast like a slow and lightly unfurled flag. I'd clipped
only a single, but important, long anchoring line, fully

ruining the entire mass of work. And it was gorgeous work.
At least thirty rows deep from the edges, engineered

over how many spider hours? All night? The day before?
The equivalent of how many constructed city blocks?

But, affixed by a single thread, another equivalent mile
down to the floor. That was a flaw. An amazing flaw.

Unforgivable in its ease of accidental sacrifice. As art can be.

How Did We Get Here?

Past all the gods, past
the potential wrath?
The eyes. Surrounded

by panels of artsy things,
cave walls, photos, hanging
organized paintings,

cut wood and steel, that nice
artificial light, plate glass,
roads and cars, society,

a spinning ball in space?
How? Were we the dare?
A punch line? The dropped call,

the scribbles or bad dream?
Or drug-induced fantasy?
An art installation arranged

in the fumble of dark or,
at last, some old and angry
man's death vision?

Aging the Dog

"And time, black dog, will sniff you out,
and lick your lean cheeks,"
　　—Charles Wright, "Future Tense"

Learn your scent and taste, absorb all your darknesses,
　　with each *tick tick* of rain working down into
the branches of the blue spruce it mistakenly tied you upon.

Black dog, I've found that place. The scarred trunk
　　　　　　　　　　　　　　　　you worked
round so long the tree has nearly died now, damaged.

The grass patch you peddled near-bare in frights of sleep,
paced down to powdery dirt.
　　　　　　　　　　But it stays on, the tree.
Body more green than blue, given faster to night's black
than when you slept here. You would not
　　　　　　　　　　　　　know it now. Time still
considers what a next move will be where you left off;

when you ran off into the ridgelines, off to the lakeshores, up
to the stone outcroppings, searching the voice
you worried it might bury while you slept, too sheltered.

　　　　　　　Tell us. What have you found since?

Savory

Palm of sand from the beach trip, ground even finer
over a year, near to dust, in a side pocket of a tote bag.
Looks like powdered sugar. Licking lips after running
in the high Arizona desert. Acridness on the tongue.
Running my hand across my arm, watching the cloud
float off. Swallowing a mouth of seawater when a wave
catches you off guard, something familiar about the taste
calling you to stay under. Watching as your mother's
saline bag drips eventually coincide with that ticking
of the wall clock's second hand. Your colleague talking
about his wife's pig-themed salt and pepper collection
fetish. Running your tongue flatly along the exposed
saddle of your lover's neck before pulling away lastly
with the tip, the bite of their taste remaining well beyond
their company. Urotherapy. It's a thing, yes. At least
it'll look like apple juice. Indian salt workers' dry hands
and feet have such high salt content, they become near
impossible to burn during cremation. Do you salt or
sugar your grits, honey? Some of the salt you've eaten
came from outer space. My sister accidentally replaced
salt for sugar in a pumpkin pie recipe one Thanksgiving.
We politely suffered through. "Chinese scramble to buy
salt as radiation fears grow." March 2011. Spilling table
salt, feeling suddenly anxious as to which hand to pinch
up the spill with and which shoulder to toss it over.
Stranded in open sea. No water. Hallucinating. Trying
to recollect an accurate definition of irony. It is proper
etiquette to pass both the salt AND pepper when asked
for only one. Other people's tears will probably not taste
as bitter as yours. The act of truly tasting them, however,
educates. Saltville is a town an hour northeast of here
famous for archeological animal finds around prehistoric
salt marshes. We once described foods as *salty,* but now
they're suddenly *savory.* I was just informed by my wife
that we've run out of salt, at which point I laughed,
informing her that I was in the middle of writing a salt poem.
That's odd timing. I told her I was not willing to travel
to China, but that Saltville was a little drive up the road.

The Call

This could be happening to everyone
for all I know, but no one lets on about it.
This *getting called back to the water,*

I'll name it. Or might it be only back
to the surface, the tossing parts.
You might disagree it's a call at all,

better recognized as a longing. A reunion.
All that fearful, bottomless salt water,
every name ever thought suspended.

Green to blue to black down to a nothing.
I am gradually wanted back out at sea,
I've suspected in these last aging years.

The boat remains in my dreams, not always
giving a pleasant rocking, the salt spray
not often pleasant to my lips; but

that my feet are only a hull separated
from eternity and my dangling fingers
dividing the foam, I seem content.

People Guessing

There are people
standing around the aisles
of fruit and vegetables, sort
of lost-looking, eyeing
the mindless melons,
rind-covered mysteries,

it seems interpreting
messages, ears down close
as fingers tap lightly,
then harder, testing a depth echo—

again, with two fingers,
then knuckles, like a knock
at a door, sure
someone's home,
the hollow stage
of sweetness
or density,
                both a lottery still—

moving on
to some other color or size
or genus of message,
roaming the interpretive landscape,

intent on finding
something akin to voice.

Handling God: Upon the Occasion
of Another Snake-handling Preacher
Killed in the Poet's Hometown

And why not Africanized bee handling?
Or Nile crocodiles? How about king cobras
or two-step adders? A box of scorpions?
A school of piranhas in the baptistery, perhaps?

You want to test God. Let's test God.

And why a big mason jar of strychnine?
Why not a line of heroin all the way up
the center aisle of the church house and out
into the gravel parking lot? Or rat poison?

You want to test God. Let's test God.

And why carbine flame dancing up your arm?
Why not about the face and eyes and mouth?
Along the frayed edges of your denim skirts?
Try smoking as you're filling your gas tank.

You want to test God. Let's test God.

Why lay on the hands? Why not medicate
from afar all the addicts and abusers. Prostitutes.
Thieves. Slumlords and death dealers. Sinners
never making it in to witness signs following?

You want to test God. Let's test God.

Why spout alien-sounding tongues even God,
the Son, and the Holy Ghost can't understand?
Why not interpret cave paintings? Or the dead
languages of gods hijacked by your religion?

You want to test God. Let's test God.

Sleepwalker

He spent the long nights
scratching shapes in the sand,

alone and not quite himself,

confessionals, barely lit
by the moon's permission,

clouds over-watching

the up-creep of waves at his back
threatening the truth

of his roughly applied rune script.

By the time he'd finally fall
again into bed, something

in him, remembered only

by morning, hoped for all
the anguish to have faded

by sun's return, the blessing

of high tide's lapping along
the shore of his middle-night's

labor accomplished. But

some etching in the shoreline
was always spared by the tide.

A hint of the dark dream.

By evening he was prompted
again by the sea. Always again.

Shadow Roaming

for Rachel

I think we trade our shadow away.
Not all at once, but in drips and motes.
Maybe at night. Is that what you feel?

That vibration of shadow's
lightness living inside and outside,
slipping away when it senses a chance

to make for the fuzzy boundary of a thing,
learning its own personality by mimicry
of anything it lands on, by memory

of things slid over in the sunlit day.
Barely anchoring a limb of itself,
still attached, to the source, sleeping,

tossing, twisting back eventually,
claiming it in the stutters of sleep spell
only a shadow would remember.

Passage

We're all thrumming our vehicles
along, like adjusted voices, through

the tunnel's white-tiled throat,
hoping in that usual morning hope

that some attentive, listening thing,
up and out there in the stoic rock,

consumes our echo of echoing
prayers tuned in slid dissonance

with every acceleration, deceleration,
as we motor on like bass-humming

Tibetan monks in harmonic chant,
winding up, searching a perfected *OM*

in the mountain's true heart, beating,
tractor-trailers and a muscle car,

my Suzuki, vibratory and convergent.

Exodus

We moved out when the house grew
into something too much to handle. Out
of what, at a glance, seems a perfectly fine place.
But it needed so much damned work,
and the animal hoarders next door,
though nice, were simply too much

to deal with, especially once the rebel flags
started flying off the porch and the cars
and the never-ending tremors of lethargy
were a poison in the air as thick
as a summer full of fifteen dogs' shit.

So we found a nicer place to rent
across town, where things quickly felt different
and still do. But I do miss
the big back yard and the garden
I started that last spring.

The unmistakable footprint of it
lingers still, reminding me how all things
shouldn't be a complete loss.
The tall brown there now is some crazed winter
morphing of last year's straight, orderly rows
and patches of once edible life—
now prettied deadheads, compostables,
weeds gone to near lighter-than-air seed.

I go by to check on the old place, feel
a cobweb brush my face, another
along the back of my hand as I walk
in through the front door. Kick a dead fly
across the linoleum.
                    The garden evidence
is still there, struggling to hold its reminder
in place, readied for another winter,
maybe wondering where we all went.

I change the thermostat over, hear
voices across the street screaming
their regular anger. It's familiar, that once
constant sound in the rank air over
the memory of fresh tomatoes and cucumbers.

New Fault Lines

In the new groove of the one bad scratch across the only song
    you really loved on that album is a day's gritty frustration,
    a valley with enough self-actualizing gravity to magnetize
    microscopic particles of the argument you were having
    when you tried lifting the player arm, but he was gripping
    your bicep with his long, bruising fingers. It's not enough
    to fill the mark left behind in the vinyl, in your arm,
    between you, through the center of what was so close
    to being a fine enough day up until everything splintered.
Snatch it up off the player with a true authority causing
    the loudest scratch you can produce, let your knee and thigh
    handle the rest of the injury, cracking into a fine finish
    a fault line across the entire glossy land of ridges. If that
    is the only control you can muster now, at this moment,
    an instant that could eventually mean everything, then
    snap that record in half already, quickly, in front of him.
Dangle the now ruined single song out there, circled in all
    that darkness, and finish destroying the loved thing.
Let him see you do it.

New Day

There's no ceremony: they just loiter
off to the sides, unnoticed, off sidewalks,
around drop-off and pick-up circles,
perhaps a few steps into the glass foyer
of hospital lobbies:
                          waiting, and waiting,
some longer than others, unable
to glance at watches that swing by
on hurried wrists, no longer able
to tell time by the direction of the sun's rays,
past all that, stricken in their new world state:

waiting, and waiting
                          for a huddled newborn
to exit the building in a loved one's arms.

Every new being needs a shadow.

The Stone's Witness

A stone, examined closely enough, is as soft as rainwater
    caught and puddled in your palm. Alive.

It can kill, with blunt force to the head, or roll
    from the mountainside, writ large and trailer-splitting.

Your gift of immovable stone is smacked open, set to force
    long ago, by God's hand, before you were born.

The red stone cries out for forgiveness. The mountains cry out.
    Even the stones of our fathers knew right from wrong.

The street stone refuses to strike the accused, rejecting
    the hand that chooses it for ideal weight and size.

Your treeless fields bloat with stumbling stones,
    eroded up with the unforgiving sadness of your children.

The well-palmed, flat stone whose only wish is to make it
    to the other bank, a dream its lost father often shared.

The foundations of your Narcissus Temple crumble
    as the earth rebels against your offset cornerstones.

Placed on the chest of an accused old man after pulled
    from the foundation of an unused colonial cabin.
    (Noted: No admission of guilt forthcoming.)

Strangely, a "stone's throw" is never thrown by the stone, is it?

May your eyes not stray from the cairns we stack in honor
    of these last days, as your names fall from monuments.

Given to the son, carried to the Holy Land,
    placed on a blood-soaked cairn in Acre three months later.

Oh, that the falling rocks might grow wings in the night,
    lifting from the children's guiltless heads that cry out.

Interchange

I interchanged the H for the V and the X for the P
on my keyboard without telling the robins this morning,

hoping a shift would come in the world, something
even I wouldn't notice, but that would settle itself out

into the language, in little lettered drops, inked-like, *tap*
and *tap-tap-tap,* like a bird's skittered but forgotten code

on a morning's tin gutter, important to it only at first, one
would think, but here now inevitably in the lasting remains

of the day, confused, or not, in a new language learned.

Just Tea Leaves

The idea that all things are connected
is both curious and daunting, that energy
is only exchanged, morphed,
rather than destroyed. Can it be
that along with all the randomness
of items in rest around us are the thousands
of hands and heads in concert, their stories
brought along with you to this moment?
That they have something to say:

This cup of green tea, the leaves grown
by someone in another country, the cream
from a cow raised by someone, milked
by someone then pasteurized by someone,
trucked, bottled, bought and brought to this café,
to a paper cup designed by someone,
manufactured by someone overseas,
made with water gathered, purified by someone
across town and jetted through water lines
manufactured and installed underground
by someone, sent through pipes installed
in this building, prepared by someone,
on equipment manufactured and purchased
by someone with currency printed by someone,
all to be set upon this table, built by someone,
where you, conceived by someone,
employed by someone, perhaps loved
by someone, now rest and drink
for a few moments, as someone.

This cup's few drops of tea carry all the potential
in the world. Everyone watches then, like ghosts,
every sip you take, guessing your next moves
and next decisions, grading your facial expressions.

The rest of so many fading lives depends on you.

Creation Theory

I was curious about the specifics of the last year, oh, so proud of what I'd ranted about out into the social ether, journaling to myself in a sense, bantering with the like-minded, occasional arguments settled only with an unfollowing or unfriending, perhaps a blocking when things really didn't go my way. I scrolled down the great wall, finding conversations, clever statements, and the like I'd all but forgotten. So many subjects I'd been emotionally invested in, I no longer cared for. I happened upon the days when I friended those I'm not speaking with in the present. A day later, and I'd rolled back time in a sense, through 2016, 2015, 2014, 2013, to that close-call run-in with 2012, and all the way to May of 2011, before my Facebook time and space gave out like a spent message sent over the pulsed light of a long-dying star. And much like the mystery of what exploded at that sudden birth of ever-expanding space made of mostly dark energy and matter, what word I chose to set off the start of this strange little mix of occasional conflict is lost to me, but it was insignificant. The tiniest of sparks. No one remains interested. Not even the creator.

You Can Start a Fire in the Woods

Knowing it lures the most curious of eyes
to size up the fire maker.

Your own nightwatch stare glowing
and darting back into the tree lines
where things hesitate in wonder.

Fire coming here only so often now.
Almost so little the animals forget
its primordial draw, the aged song. But

it comes back, so long as a single being
picks up the scent, gives the others that look
of remembrance, close to a grin,
that it's probably all right to go nearer
now, toward the light, there,
where it flickers tall in the clearing.

Where the fire maker crouches, staring.

Staring at the eyes arriving, one
after another, another, in the floating black,
blinking orange and yellow, like waking
stars having fallen, that wait to fully wake
now for you there, a step closer,
though they would have you
remain still and wonder.

They want to know about you
as much as you want to know about them.

Both afraid. Both trying to remember
a fear of fire from a time before.

A New Comfort

I will take my last personal day soon.
Then there's a good chance every day
after that will be a personal day for a while,
a long job now over for a long time, maybe.
Finally a break from years of red-tape-strangled,
paranoid higher ed admin bureaucracy,
the job's secret mission to kill so many
of us off as loudly and messily as possible.

I claimed once I wanted to *not know what
it is I am to do next.* I probably meant it.

I'd lost comfort in the schedule of living.
Grown to mistrust the mechanics of how
everything found its way into life,
onto calendars, lifelessly.
                                   How the wrong
people pulled those itchy strings. How
all the wrong reasons dictated what I did
and what I was expected to think. At least
that's how the game I was losing felt.

Something shifted, finally. Jabbed me.
The Universe yawned its gigantic *O*-shaped
lips, sounding out what I think I recognized
as the old word: *Opportunity.*
                                   Not the corporate,
soulless sort, but the word's truest origin,
back into the sound's intent, to an instance
of use, before the Sumerian equivalent
was pressed into soft clay, long back
when a cliff dweller peeked out of his cave
one morning and noticed, for the first time,
a thing so much more than just a sunrise.

A Carving Time

Do you sense the humming
of hesitation, just as the knife
breaks the toughness of rind,
that wonder whether the stubbornness
comes more from the orange-spined shell
of the pumpkin or from your own
testing grip of the twisting blade?

But something does finally give
and slices down, doesn't it,
deep into the pulpy gourd,
filling the air with a sudden autumn,
a forced sawing commencing,
the Jack-o'-Lantern's smile
forming as you struggle
and grimace against the flesh.

A Particular Instant

He scanned the past for a moment,
just one, when things first made the least sense.

Some of us crave that certain knowing
of when it all comes together for us,
for good, a first perfect moment of least effort
when the world turns in our favor,
wanting only the best for us.

When the all-seeing eyes grant wishes
we didn't even know we wanted.

But now, Franky was caught up wondering
the opposite, about when things
had gone so horribly bad for the first time,
unraveled deliberately against his betterment.

Were such instances easy to recognize
in retrospect, might others see them more easily?
Had he even been warned, been given advice
he'd ignored? Been so very blind?

Were there vast conspiracies in the world
with his name etched on them
as a form of entertainment for some unnamed entity
watching over his regular adversity?
A scourge named after only him: Franky's Curse.

But after so much studying on the formula
that was the uncomfortable timeline of his life,
all Franky could come up with
was the night he was born.

And that made him feel quite special.

To Go Look Soon

There are leaves out on the ground,
on the gravel of the driveways,
along the alley and main road, lodged
in the hedgerows and emptied limbs: waiting.

Each deserves a little inspection of its own
and knows it, senses a curiosity hanging
like some next shift of air studying on where
to make important things happen.

One particular leaf, a river delta
of veiny white grown over sunburst orange,
tips still sharp as sewing pins, is buried
under a mat of last night's browning carpet,

promises to hold on out there
only so much longer now. Nothing waits
for nothing in the weight of a season's press
of the clock, when rot is the day's color.

This Hanging On

after Ron Houchin's "World of the Dead"

I thought once: It is a recruiting of throats and lungs
for speaking in sleep, or walking with their feet,
hiding belongings as if they still belonged to you.

This is the drawn-out argument we have with death.
Determinedly unconvinced, hitching rides on others,
on the insides. In this chapter we're inhabited thickly

with the living, an inter-veiling and so strangely close
as to speak to one another in the same voice at times,
interrupting in mirrors, a glance just too familiar

in some of the aged photos mostly forgotten. No
one explains if it's a choice made to hang around,
this infiltration of another's days. Who would truly

want such a thing, even in death? A constant reunion.

An Endurance III

For the sake of 150-mile-an-hour winds testing palm trees
you leaned on only a month ago, we endure.

For the sake of panic attacks at a time in life
when you've "never felt better," we endure.

For the sake of that same solid white feral cat
that slinks through the back yard every morning
while you're drinking your first cup of coffee, we endure.

For the sake of your last, last confession, we endure.

For the sake of unfinished cups of coffee found in the console of the
car on a cold morning, and wondering how many days old they are
before taking a chance just for the extra caffeine boost, we endure.

For the sake of the mystery of always having more mosquito bites
than everyone else during picnics out by the river, we endure.

For the sake of yet another scam call about the warranty
on the used car you gave your sister three years ago, we endure.

For the sake of the mason jar full of change, labeled "Florida Trip,"
you found in an abandoned house but are still too afraid
to cash in, we endure.

For the sake of the one tree you left alone
to grow when it sprouted in the middle of the yard
when you missed a mowing,
                              we endure.

Dawn to Dusk

And outside it's raining, light enough
so drips from gutters and eves are louder
than the rainfall. When it quits
for a bit, the drops keep on the *ticktock*
rhythm of a determined high-heeled woman
making her quick way along a sidewalk
with that not-so-subtle stride punctuated
with a clacking you might feel,
if you're close enough, through the asphalt
into your own feet, up through the vibrations
of the car as you idle at the intersection,
mistaking that new tapping as a miss
in your engine,
                              a problem the garage guys
won't find when you take it in for a checkup,
all of them looking at you strangely
as you try impersonating the odd culprit noise.
It begins storming as you're driving home
after work. You have no umbrella.
You find some relaxation in the rhythm
of the back-and-forth of the windshield wipers,
notice how they would cause a faint alteration
in the car's direction with each sweeping arc
if you were to let go of the steering wheel.
The mystery noise from earlier is gone.

I Like How It Can Be Raining

without being obvious, the normal cloudiness
keeping normal secrets. I like how the sun
can shine down through slanted rain,
unexpectedly, as if each drop is lit
for a little while, near blinding in its strobe,
like the arrival of an alien event in the middle of the day
every new time it happens, that sheet of crystals
careening from the sky:
                              making you wonder how
can we have it this way, rain and sun together,
or deserve the gift of this strangeness, the same
as standing still under an awning during a storm,
yet hurtling through the question of space.

What Is This Complete Exhaustion

of the spirit? How deep does the pain
of the mind penetrate to the heart,
set up in the spirit to slow its beating,
begin dulling the eyes from sparkle?

Here is a great parade of heartbreak,
the endless grunts of bother, every
glance a reminder of mortality,
as I sip my coffee on the same café
barstool as before: knee replacements,
heart catheterizations and stents,
open heart valve replacement, now
this dislocated and broken shoulder.
Bless her heart. Bless all our hearts.
I grow too used to this place, I think.

No one enters the hospital chapel.
Or even seems to come near it.
It's too near the constant traffic vein,
hardly noticeable. Still, the prayer
request journal sits open and heavy

with ink, a quieted book full of years
of pleading for life and endings
of suffering,
                        for answers. I wonder
how the hell the stand holds such
a burden upright without collapsing
under the weight of those questions.

Perhaps we're all lightening the load
as we pass, just the slightest right bit
without knowing. Is that part
of an unwritten agreement
we have no need of knowing?

        That we pass around the weight
        of prayers as some kind of spell
        to dissipate our unspeakable burdens?

Fading Illuminations

for David McDonald

Now, these many years later, something
akin to a sage ghost surfaces in the books
he donated to the library when he lived,
before passing in wait for that donated heart.

These might have been given by his estate.
Or in some mysterious trek-finding way
to the research stacks from boxed-up shelves
when someone finally occupied his office.

I recognize his handwriting at once. Surely
I'd received sufficient marked papers
back then—the subjects, philosophy and history—
for that, his instruction wanting more effort,
more understanding of the lessons.

Marginal notes, his scribbles, decipherable
only to me now, I imagine, the aging student
of the phantom professor roaming, not old halls,
but a mind by way of deteriorating, forgotten
books I pick up for a quarter each at the library.

I reminisce in these occasional conversations.
Lectures from yellowed, brittle forms:
underlinings, parenthetical references, circles
and arrows, exclamation points, highlights,
dog-eared pages, simple reiterations of thought.

What does the past truly instruct of the future?

Is he questioning himself? I feel in the remark
an aura of disillusionment, jotted down
long before any first bouts of heart failure
and society's proving out of an answer
to his marginal musing: It is true, I think,
We learn from history, nothing from history.

We should better pay attention to its ghosts.

Invocation

Smooth, blue-hued marble Mary,
pray for us in our days of confusion,
in these days we have yet to name
for fear of truth and retribution.

Mary P., Barista of St. Starbucks,
two-year employee of the hospital
vending service, who is always
on your feet and moving, pray for us
in our late evening hour of fatigue.

Mary (LNU), pray for yourself
as we pray for you, at three
in the morning while emptying
the eternalness of hazmat bags.

Mary, mother of my being, root
of my breathing and blood, we pray
for you in your hour of morphine
IV drip, X-rays, and CT scans.

Moon's Dance

Never commit falsities
on a blood-red full moon
in the dead of winter.

The moon knows lies
when she hears them,
even through the haze
of clouds hinting snow
before sunrise.

Some winter airs
are a clear thing,
thinly lofted and shrewd.

Why expose your heart
to such a night blindness?
Why disappoint
the dark with doubt?
Confound inwardly.

Force her hand;
make her reveal who
and what you really are,
whether shrinking in night
or in day, behind
stone or cowered
in storms, shipbound
or growing blind
in your own grave.

You are known.
And all you've done.

Bad Coffee

You shouldn't have to drink bad coffee.
But for every cup of shitty coffee there is a misery
to match, so we let coffee go bad, making it badly,
even when we don't have to. It cools in the pot,
overcooks, boils and percolates, burns all day
and night at the diner; decaf keeps being made,
along with instant. We sip the half cup of cold mess
we left in the car overnight, cringing with every
swallow, loving the company of another lurch
to come, that chewy grit at the bottom of the cup,
bittered. We let people keep making weak coffee
at work, smile when sipping another awful cup
out of politeness, refuse to send it back at a café.
It's nice to place that taste of misery we sometimes
only get to think on for a time, inviting to walk
into a place where you can feel it in the smoky air
and know there's some satisfaction there to be
anticipated in a cup with a taste you can name.

Not a Man of the Bog

This was not a Heaney-like
tight hug of bog mud,
an accidentally perfect spot
to encapsulate, that would

have kept me, preserving
my fishing gear and whatever
final look on my struggling
face might have been. No,

being a river bank
and solid under my boots
until that second I sunk,
both legs to the mid-thighs,

the next flood, which came
often enough and which
created this consuming
pit of quicksand,

would have washed me
away, miles downstream,
unkept, damaged, destined
to be no famed bog man

but an eventually mangled
thing, rolled up on a shore
who knows where,
detached from my homeland,

or forever caught quick
by an under-rock,
one day finally consumed
by minnows and giant catfish.

Autumn, and the Season Shifts

in shallow hides, as senses flare
with every shiver-spill invited
up our spines, across the scalp,

behind the eyes
                and burning minds,
communed in patience, waiting
for the color drop and blanketing
of beddings long forgotten, still

to greet their tired and itching
soilish fingers torn from stilling hearts,
with splitting tongues in atrophy
persisting
          with your face in mind.

When passing graves on Hallowed Nights
and clickish voice of a crow is caught
up in the wind,
          you probably should run
and heed its call. Make scarce yourself,

or otherwise stay on to bear
some witness, beasts that claw away
from sleepless heaps intent to take you
on their backs and fly to where

blood never ends,
          blood never ends.

Betiding

I gather found items for the great tide
of divining I feel surely comes. What speaks up
from the ground, from an innocent kitchen table,
a stranger's shelves. A cedar chest across town.

Some especially for what daylight betides,
some for a dark's only messaging. All choosing
their own work when tossed downward like stony runes
taking on the mantle of new lives:
                                        a gold finger bone,
a brother to the mud, pulled from a river's fickle edge
after a hundred-year flood, a blue fading feather
found floating along on a summer hot backroad,
a page of the Old and of the New Testament, folded
correctly, soaked between a lying virgin's cheek
and gum like a chaw of tobacco, not near as sweet.

All of it bundled up tightly by a secret cut
of ex-lover's bedhead hair and buried a foot deep
in Tennessee clay on a ripe moon.
                                        I'll leave it

there, unsure of how long to let the song root and grow
so wildly, rounding like an animal egg. Swelling full
of the familiar work of hands above ground.

            In the light, in the wind,

where I can better count out my numbered days.

Another Winter

I've not worried much
about sleeping in the house
since they broke in

almost three years ago,
taking everything of worth
to me, those few heavy

handfuls. I haven't slept
in the house since, and I put it
up for sale immediately

with not a bit of luck,
every prospective buyer
suspecting some trouble,

perhaps from the desperate
look I try to hide in my eyes.

Haunted? Why, yes, it is.

In every way you might
imagine, this place, it is haunted.
There was a murder here.

Things moan and creak.
There are voices that never cease.
The house is burdened

with a broken spirit
too emptied of poetry to vacate
the cave of its own heart.

Sweet Potato Lore #1

Plant one extra slip for every three you desire to live, a fine and healthy one—and don't be stingy with this sacrifice, child. Plant on the evening of a promised full moon, but don't spy her that night, though you're tempted, even if called to speak of things only the night should hear. Take an antique photo of a couple you've never met, bartered without money from an antique shop, torn in half at their shoulders, tossed into the soil and fully covered—one on one end of the crop mounds, one on the other—so their whispers thread the soils all summer long. Choose well an uneaten specimen from last harvest's crop, sprouted inside your home in the dark where you thrive, wrapped and unspied by anyone. Plant it whole-bodied in the center of the potato mound field. Stake the spot. Let this lovely mess of vines grow high and wild, all the loosed leafed eyes in watch for the first killing frost.

Running the Optics

One.

If some machine could be hooked to your mind,
your eyes, result in some remarkable retracing
of lifelong patterns of glances, of prolonged foci,
the halfway points of meditation and peripheral glimpses,

how much more would you regret having lived,
perceiving newly the near endlessness of visible paths
over innocence and guilt to which you were both
witness and primary party?
                                        All might be clear to you:
where it all went odd. The spots vibrating in a way
only you might recognize, red-hot indications
like on an old-style computer board gone strange
and flashy, resembling neon-lit subway stops. *Here,*

here: you should have said no. *Here* you might have
only gone halfway. *There.* That was a terrible thing
to do. Oh, to have turned around *about there,* yes?

Two.

The art opening was visually overwhelming.
A two-artist show, their work was a series
of nine-by-twelve-inch watercolor and inks
relating to surreal animals in absurd scenes:

juggling bears and birds driving cars, clown
jackalopes, marching deer bands on parade.

A West Coast artist began by sending a first
piece to the other artist out east who then
created a new piece as inspired from the first,
and so on, each painting related to the next
and next until they'd generated a full gallery.

The show was installed in no obvious order,
but we followed the chronological timeline

of inspiration, painting to painting to painting,
by colored string strung overhead, the string
itself inadvertently inventing another work.

There was no mention of how the positions
of each work were chosen, or the string colors.
Or the distances between works. Or a number
of days between paintings agreed upon, or
of a limited number of subject materials used.

What remained unstated along the in-between
outweighed the show itself, and I was left
wondering if I'd missed some other room, or
if I was due a guide offering further explanation.

Three.

Or—see what you've neglected
by way of the massive sinkholes

you awake to one morning,
suddenly self-aware, or, needing

the nudge, watch footage of a city block
sunken deep into an amazingly

unreal overhead black round crispness, or
lost in smoky crumbles

like a concrete Atlantis across the news
over your coffee and cereal, some

element of the scene, the lingering violence
familiar past any usual empathy you enjoy.

Watch as no one stirs down there
from the helicopter vantage point.

Nothing appears to move
within the wreckage,

like the aftermath of a plane disaster
on a mountainside. This is your doing.

Well past cleaning up and losing
good sleep over. The blood cord is cut;

your guilt is so much a part of who
you've become. Turn to the wanted ads

in the paper: *Good Fill Dirt—$50 a ton.*
Not a bad deal, you think. You switch

off the television, go to the fridge
to put away the almond milk and forget

what you were thinking on, and head out
for work to go fight morning traffic.

Four.

Pick your bread.

A type of bread
that sets up, hardens
nicely in the dry day

as you walk, chunks off
and chips into visible crumbs,
sizable enough,
tough enough,

to choke and frustrate
the hungriest birds,
so they'll leave
your hopeful trail backward
out of the terrible decisions alone.

Cumberland & 20th Street

Late winter, just between warm and cool
enough to roll my windows down to let some
real wind in after these months of cooped up
recirculated funk, even if what's rushing in
now to replace it is the day's air swirled
with puffs of diesel fume and engine rumble.
This is the town's longest intersection. We're all
waiting, feet on brakes, clutches to the floor,
the stress of flexed legs, finger grips and stares
eye-balling red lights ahead like an eddied river
of tight-wound choreographed springs in wait,
only to surge to the next intersection.

Most windows are up, but mine being down
gives me a better view, and I have a habit
of breaking the rule of traffic privacy.
I trust the looks will come. They're tempted,
quick flashes from the corners of eyes,
from rearview and side-mirror glances,
but no such commitment as a head turn. Never.
That would reveal too much. Like how days begin.
The rest of it, their plans, how it's all falling apart.
The shallow breathing setting in, the crow's feet
from squinting, the yet-unidentified pain in the back,
the ignored pile of tossed bills in the backseat.

What else is daydreamed on now at this metaphor
of a juncture, this true juncture, this aggravating
standstill, this traffic jam, this damned red light
that just won't let go, this reminder of mortality
in these cages of glass and steel. I could go on,
but then there are smiles. Of course, the smiles.
It's not all jacked up and ruined at this hot spot
of asphalt reckoning no one bothers to look at.

Some are happy loitering here in their cars, not
just smiling when finally allowed to course on
by the tricolored hanging robots. Some, at least.

Who knows what will come to mind by the next
red light for others. Good things, maybe...let's hope.
To tempt them to look over, then grin. Perhaps
when it's my turn to get caught daydreaming.

Somewhere in the Days

If the title of a collection is somewhere
found phrased in the poems,
then maybe the title of a life is somewhere
scattered in its days, if that sort of thing

interests you. Don't look for the glanced label
at the top, as it were. Or the beginning, if you're
making amends or starting over. Or both.

How do we know our forbearers
haven't thought ahead and named us
long ago, and not just by some
enumerated or nicknamed generation:

                    solved by

    x,
    or *y,*
    or *millennial,*
    beat,
    greatest,
    boomer, or
    lost.

I'm Resigned to It

Finally.

Who and what they are, where
they're from, is hard to tell.

But they're light, I know. Pure light.

After all this time, all these years
of questions, that inevitable journey looms
like a planet's last sunset.

A long, welcomed, beautiful looming.

But it's hard to tell what's true.
What's true and what's not anymore.
Hard to tell what I'm saying
or thinking: Is this a conversation
or just us staring into another's eyes,
praying for connection?
            For light.

All the languages, everything
passing for language and its rules,
merged into that one deep
penetrating maelstrom of knowledge.

That's why
        we built up. And up.

You won't remember most things
but, rest assured, you
were the epitome of accomplishment
in the face of ignorance.

When you are again
wondering in the womb,
relearning all things muffled
by the egg and skin, this
is what will swirl in your mind
as a type of déjà vu:

preferences, wishes, afterthoughts.

Remembrances of shades of light.

A part of you will know this,
even in the midst of your suffering
and loving in the next turn
of the wheel.

It's what you wanted.
What you needed.
It was the good medicine
you required. And the love you find
and give, that's just extra.

You can have and give
as much of that as you like. It's free.

As never-ending as the stars.
        As never-ending as light.

But you'll suffer a little, too,
along the wide path. You wished it that way.

There's so much you could do: Run
like the water. Live in the trees
as wind. Be the first emerging amphibian
to suck up air. Feel the thumping rush
of a lion's heart in your chest.

You might be the bedrock foundation
of a cathedral. Or the patient, grotesque
gargoyle on its roof line.

Or the last krill to be swallowed up
by the last whale. How about
the last remaining bullet fired
by the last remaining gun?
The last of a last of a last anything.

A mad genius, only appreciated
a hundred years after your death.

A filthy rich, crazed, egocentric narcissist
no one remembers but by your rusting name
on a decrepit building giggling children
pass under every morning without
the slightest curiosity.

The first drop of water
on a thirsty man's tongue.
         Poison.

It's all there in the dark and the light.

Move in closer. Choose. Choose
which column of light to ride into the dark.
Past the stars. Into their collapsing hearts.

Name which diversion of prophesy
you'll ride upon as the truth of the night.

Name it:
        first child, supernova, an absence of light.

A Simple Cup of Coffee Out on the Deck

There's a light rain. It was clear yesterday.
Before that it rained for six straight days.
Fresh water from the sky. Fresh and clean,
like now, clicking on the awning, the deck wood,
the too-saturated ground, the out-of-control grass,
out on the highway.
                                And isn't California
still in drought? How long can that actually last?
What qualifies as environmental famine eventually?
What would that landscape out there look like?
Isn't desertification fascinating and frightening
all at once?
                        And why does desalinization
have to cost so damn much when you're suffering
and staring right at an entire ocean? Your feet
in the water of its shores. A desert filled
with solar panels would solve it all. But why
the greed? Is it really as simple and as complicated
as that? Why the greed about anything?

And I wonder what the names are of the women
walking miles a day for a few buckets
of barely clean water in African countries.

I Don't Know When It Fell, the Top

half of the tree, in dark or light.
But it's down now, mostly dismantled,
there across the almost always quiet field,

like a new nest of gigantic twigs,
half assembled, the exposed insides
of cracked limbs soft and white in the day.

Bright red cardinal males
along with their warm brown mates
have commenced to finding comfort

in the lower branches of the mess already.
I hope the owner of the field finds it
in his heart to just leave the branches

alone where they've fallen.

Caught in Barbed Wire

The obligatory blue plastic grocery bag, tattered,
an overworked handle stretched and broken,
a hint as to why it was first lost.

Where a young spider randomly landed
after letting out webbing in a gust of wind,
caught up like a parachute to see the world.
Now setting up a first home at the corner
of rusting steel wire and a rotting wood post.

A strip of yellow ribbon, threadbare,
red dirt-stained, a portion of the past bow
intact, from one of a hundred graves
decorated with fake flowers
from the cemetery down the lane.

Tuft of hair yanked from a living hide.

Nail, twisted and dangling, willed out
of the tree's bark by the tug and pull
of the old oak's years of widening
and the finite tightening of wire.

A difference between sun-lit wire
and what is shadowed. The one, lightened
grayish, the other, reddish and browned,
an amount of rust contributing variance.

New honeysuckle vine grasping tendrils
from lower wires up to the next like
rising notes to be played in coming yellow blooms.

A singing of quickened late winter air
along the lines, like over-strung instrument strings,
optimistic the whole arrangement will hold
in their infinitesimal years of tightening.
The note raised half of a half of a tone
since this time last year and after the kudzu
died back enough.
                        Quit deadening the song.

Weather Report

Pick certain vegetables
as a storm brews,
if pluckiness is your thing.

Sweet potato, onion, low tomatoes,
the in-betweens and such,
on your knees, braving what stirs, lords above.

Calmly race the rains.

Disturb the ground before it's too wet to handle;
squeeze and snap the limbish vine;
listen to the protest glee, daring, and thunder.

Ignore splats on your neck,
skin reddened from the day.
The storm doesn't care.

Why should you? And have you tasted
the day through your knees yet?
As it lifts voice. Lifts song.

Dig your toes in, then.
Find beets. Fill your pockets, son.
The basket's done in.

As the Crow Flies

No crow flies straight, after all.
They enjoy other means of navigation
besides clever human phrases.
We should wonder what a crow
calls out for when in the midst of flight.
What conversation can't wait
until a limb or line? It's understandable
their kind would call out mid-winged
on the wind for advice, wondering which way,
and, failing to see another, at least glide
to familiarity if answered. But,
if not, what then makes for navigable
decision-making, other than hunger's pain
and company?
          I think they enjoy connecting
the dots as much as we did as children.
But for them, it might be black roof to black roof,
the sweeping chimney smoke, azimuths
set from graveyards to lone hilltop trees
with histories, or chopped mountain tops
reddened with no trees. Flight here is a constancy
with green on green, the darks and missing
darks the only daylight guides.

And who among us walks straight
when finding ourselves in an open field? None,
I'd think. We would meander, curious
in relaxed weavings, letting the feet speak
with the ground more than being led
by the want of eyes, like I can imagine
unhurried, lonely black wings do
on the mindless winds.

Prophesy, Lament

One.

The evening bleeds again its finest reds
between dry silhouettes of perfect winter

branches, our appetites for wind-blood
wide-eyed, never satisfied, sky scene silent

but for murmurating red-winged blackbirds
dancing waves through scarlet-orange drapery,

forcing us to wonder if such uncommon color
will be a last vision or sign of things to come.

Two.

The sun, twilight backward echoing,
an animal out there, like some distant

lone howl of a dog barely caught behind
highway traffic. Then another, lamenting

a dying day that cannot speak for itself
but calls on the small offerings at sunset,

combining into some creature with snarls
as the last sliver of sun sizzles away.

Emptied

for Henry

We lifted you up in loving howls
last night, you should know,

to a near-full, slight gibbous moon,
your ancient, near-deaf ears perked

curiously at our racket around the fire,

emptying our small breaking hearts
up through our throats in the best

half-language we could manage,
straining out that forestalling grief.

And after you were finally gone,
exhaled your stubborn last,

tonight the storms came, light in the sky,

pulsing quiet until time for the winds
to howl in and the thunder to catch up,

and we fancied it a mighty gift
from wherever you were

out and up there, tearing at the night.

Unreliable

But this is what dreams do. Lie. Lie like they hate you.
Exaggerate. Woo you quiet, like a trusted hand's caress
of the fevered forehead. Hum those familiar lullabies.

You grope the space, even try smelling what waits there
just beyond the tips of your fingers, there in that most
frightening of darknesses.
                    But you back out, cave-frightened.

Forgetting the words. The tune. Nothing waits. Nothing
prefers you. Nothing clambers after your notions after all.

Nothing is the undefinable dark. Its only wish is to fill
the spaces with a chaos of awe. To astound. Mindlessly.

Effortlessly. You're merely a vessel. You speak messages
without knowing, when dreaming your déjà vu flashes
of awareness. Your thick-filled scarlet heart, electric-pulsing
mind, artificially swirling thoughts adding up to memory.

Your encasing skull. Time capsule instances of moments,
all hard-wired to the eyes, those lovely untrustable eyes.

This is what dreams do. Lie. This is what dreams do, liar.

Affinity

The only animal I dream of is the crow. Others are surely in there, arguing for time on the sleepy stage. Maybe dancing elephants on marbles, a surprisingly calm conversation between sharks as they circle in on the trails of fresh blood, or some dogs in clown suits playing cards and erupting into a sword fight (they shout in Croatian, subtitled with Viking runes and neon cave drawings), but I don't remember them. Only the persistent crow manages to remain perched off a branch of my waking, calling out its versed demands, snapping my spine straight with its taunts. Its swoops over my head keep me agitated among the word-hunting fields, promising its message, its lofty gifts. Some muse shadowed in the tree line, too shy to step out into true light. Its dark flights past sundown when I'm blinded and without words. What would I do without such a friend?

Surprised with Crystal

April flakes wind-dance
cherry blossom trees
lining the slow night road,
streetlamps lending a lit
focus invisible by day.

Early morning walk
where no one has disturbed,
my steps lead me under
these trees that were only
just giving thought to bloom.

> Crystallized snow tufts
> seem practice blooms caught nested
> in the pronged branches.

The pink petal hints
stain the ice and snow,
having gripped and soaked all night,
and, if given necessary attention,
mirror the colors of sunrise.

Fogs Fall

Having fled the cratered fog, now safely hugged
by the southern shadows of Cumberland's ridges,
the gap-saddled greetings of mornings ensued
and lighter grew the days since fleeing the crater;
sounds of struggle still echoed in the basin of home,
though little thought was granted by me of how
the wolves had progressed in their long assault
on sanity and of a town's long-exhausted dreams.

But the fogs, trapped, with minds of their own,
woke, hating their geostatic station and, urged on
by subtle northern winds, reversed and turned,
spinning their white ghosts, light enough to escape
the crater, unheavied enough to seek the tunnel,
demanding some permanent escape from this hole
of a town, knowing life dwelt away from there;

the mountain dam of earth bursting the early dark
of morning, loosing wispy desperation; a shot
of sky—of sun-killing weapons of apathy, death,
remembering us—set the old ancient wilderness
trail in place again, calling our many lost names.

The Source

We keep a barrel of heartbreak buried
in the layered bog of our chests,

a history of histories held fast

by ribs of fallen branches, the gallons
of tears welling up and waiting,

a tipping point edged over
when least expected, so inconveniently,

by a simple word, a glance of light,

the quiet whispered leak from what's dammed
behind polite laughter within the scent

of mood-tides barely kept, a traded smile
along the street, out in the tragic airs

we can't help but breathe up in quick gasps.

Acknowledgments

American Journal of Poetry: "Enter the Feasts"
Third Wednesday: "In Timing"
Arkana: "Justness"
Spillway: "An Enduring"
The Ibis Head Review: "Creation Theory"
Nature Writing: "To Go Look Soon"
Mockingheart Review: "This Hanging On"
Dead King Magazine: "Bad Coffee"
Slattery's Art of Horror: "Remains"
Sweater Weather: "Another Winter," "Surprised with Crystal"
Paper Plane Pilots: "Cumberland & 20th Street"
Full of Crow: "Affinity"
Three Drops from a Cauldron: "Sweet Potato Lore #1"
Kaaterskill Basin Literary Journal: "Fogs Fall"

About FutureCycle Press

FutureCycle Press is dedicated to publishing lasting English-language poetry books, chapbooks, and anthologies in both print-on-demand and Kindle ebook formats. Founded in 2007 by long-time independent editor/publishers and partners Diane Kistner and Robert S. King, the press incorporated as a nonprofit in 2012. A number of our editors are distinguished poets and writers in their own right, and we have been actively involved in the small press movement going back to the early seventies.

The FutureCycle Poetry Book Prize and honorarium is awarded annually for the best full-length volume of poetry we publish in a calendar year. Introduced in 2013, our Good Works projects are anthologies devoted to issues of universal significance, with all proceeds donated to a related worthy cause. Our Selected Poems series highlights contemporary poets with a substantial body of work to their credit; with this series we strive to resurrect work that has had limited distribution and is now out of print.

We are dedicated to giving all of the authors we publish the care their work deserves, making our catalog of titles the most diverse and distinguished it can be, and paying forward any earnings to fund more great books.

We've learned a few things about independent publishing over the years. We've also evolved a unique, resilient publishing model that allows us to focus mainly on vetting and preserving for posterity poetry collections of exceptional quality without becoming overwhelmed with bookkeeping and mailing, fundraising activities, or taxing editorial and production "bubbles." To find out more about what we are doing, come see us at www.futurecycle.org.

The FutureCycle Poetry Book Prize

All full-length volumes of poetry published by FutureCycle Press in a given calendar year are considered for the annual FutureCycle Poetry Book Prize. This allows us to consider each submission on its own merits, outside of the context of a contest. Too, the judges see the finished book, which will have benefitted from the beautiful book design and strong editorial gloss we are famous for.

The book ranked the best in judging is announced as the prize-winner in the subsequent year. There is no fixed monetary award; instead, the winning poet receives an honorarium of 20% of the total net royalties from all poetry books and chapbooks the press sold online in the year the winning book was published. The winner is also accorded the honor of being on the panel of judges for the next year's competition; all judges receive copies of all contending books to keep for their personal library.

www.ingramcontent.com/pod-product-compliance
Lightning Source LLC
Chambersburg PA
CBHW070006100426
42741CB00012B/3123